KOKUMO ROCKS was born in Dundee in 1965, but was raised in the Fife mining village of Cowdenbeath. Hers was the only black family in the area, and she left school with no qualifications or spelling. It wasn't until she attended university in the mid-'90s that she was diagnosed as dyslexic. In 1991 she decided to change the direction of her life following a near-death experience, and began to fulfil her life-long ambition to become a performance poet. Kokumo's poetry explores the themes of love, race, freedom and imprisonment, and she does so with a sense of the importance of fun and humour – proud to include 'the flabby bits'. She describes herself as an African/Asian/Scottish writer and performance poet, and has performed in the UK, USA, India and Africa. Kokumo – the name means 'this one will not die' – lives by the motto 'if you don't ask you won't get', and believes that passion can turn the 'mundane into excitement'. She has been inspired by poets including Maya Angelou, Benjamin Zephaniah and Ivor Cutler, but above all by 'growing up black in Scotland'.

By the same author:

Bad Ass Raindrop, Luath Press, 2002
Stolen From Africa, Luath Press, 2007

Happily Drowning

KOKUMO ROCKS

Luath Press Limited
EDINBURGH
www.luath.co.uk

First published 2018

ISBN: 978-1-912147-15-1

The author's right to be identified as author of this book
under the Copyright, Designs and Patents Act 1988 has been asserted.

The paper used in this book is recyclable. It is made
from low chlorine pulps produced in a low energy, low emission
manner from renewable forests.

Printed and bound by Ashford Colour Press, Gosport

Typeset in 11 point Sabon

© Kokumo Rocks 2018

From a very proud grandma
to her wonderful newborn grandson,
Harry Patrick Rocks,
who arrived on Monday 22 October 2018

Contents

Preface	9
Bella's Gate	11
Snow Biting	12
Hello Sunshine	13
Yellow Bird	14
The Gilt Mirror	15
Am I a Fish?	16
In the Face of Madness (age five)	17
Guardian Moon	18
A Moon Morning	19
Ti Amo Rain	20
Fly or Die	21
Happy	22
Happily Drowning (in Crete)	23
Dangling Legs (In Stromness)	25
Cherubs' Needs	26
Rainbow Hands (in Princes Street)	27
Trust	28
Morning Delight	30
He Threw the Dice	31
Today is Not a Good Day (definitely not)	32
Wet Socks in Leith	34
Demented Ironing Board	35

Sulphur-scented Haggis	36
What on Earth Happened? (in Mallaig)	37
Screaming in Ecstasy	39
Warm and Toasty (in Princes Street)	41
Tiny Blue Flower	42
Ghost Trees	43
No End Road	44
The Moon in Brazil	45
Wise Woman	46
The VIP Letter	47
The Fringe Festival	48
Creatures	50
Today	51
Today I Woke Up	52
Suck Out the Juice	53
Ice Tea	54
Visions of Scotland	55
Winking Fairy	56
Night Market in Lagos	57
Girl Power	59
What is a Logophile?	60
Nazareth House (prison aged six)	61
Obama Inauguration	62
Bring Back Our Girls	65
The Glassy Loch	66
Shy Love's Blush	67
Hurrah I'm in the Club	68
Dreamscape Melts	70

Preface

THE POEMS IN this collection reflect journeys I have taken along routes I never expected to travel – or even knew existed. I have found myself searching for answers to questions I hadn't thought of in my conscious mind ever before. The title arose from a life-changing experience I had on holiday in Crete last year. I got into difficulties on a motorised raft, pulled the throttle and slipped overboard. As I sank deeper and deeper, instead of panic or fear, my sensation was of floating unhurriedly, enjoying the silence, keenly aware of the vivid blueness of the sea; there was a feeling of contentment in letting go of life and accepting death. Then something jolted my brain and I shot up to the surface.

For me, the poems in *Happily Drowning* represent my unconscious search for the serenity and stillness of that near-death experience – but now I want to find it in life, grounded on this earth – even more so in the light of my brother's unexpected death while I was working on this collection.

In 'Screaming in Ecstasy' I write: 'I am all yours, rich earth. Enfold me. Cover my body beneath your soil… I shoot out of the ground, uprooting trees… Till I land naked… rebirthed anew.' Through expressions of my sensuous love of life in the natural world, I am asking: where do we go after we die? 'Fly or Die' also raises the issue of the existence of spirit and my connectedness to it. In 'Trust': 'A goddess stood on the windowsill, watching… I'm scared, have doubts.' Could I trust this figure with her outstretched hand? Should I go to her and would I find the contentment and serenity I had been searching for? My love for the natural world has guided me in this exploration. In 'The Glassy Lochs', 'I gasp at this ethereal sight harbouring snow-capped mountains within its grasp... I sink down and I cry and cry.' The sublime spirit of Scotland's natural landscape has often moved me to tears. In 'Ghost Tree', 'the forest has sumptuous, sensuous textures. Rough as dog's teeth... fungi soft as down.'

In turning to Scotland's wild beauty, rich language and rebellious spirit for inspiration, I have made the breathtaking discovery of it as an expression of *who I am*. Scotland, my home, has become part of my inner landscape in such a way that I have integrated all three parts of my identity – my African, Asian and Scottish selves.

In *Happily Drowning*, I reveal part of me I don't often share with others, or explore as a performance poet (what about my street cred!). Publicly exposing my longing for something higher than myself is not easy. Huge thanks to Nick Thorpe for all of his support and the support of my many good friends who know who they are.

Writing these poems has been a process of divining self through intimate reflections on the natural world and asking questions, often unknowingly, about the meaning of life and death. In so doing I have journeyed closer to a more complete self, where that stillness, serenity and contentment I yearn for has found a place. So here they are to share with you.

Kokumo Rocks
November 2018

Bella's Gate

Bella's gate swung melodiously
sweeping over the long grass
while the wind salsaed
the padlock rattled
adding percussion to the gate's song.

Snow Biting

Floating flakes
birling to the ground
I stick out my tongue
catch one – melts, gone.
I try another and some more
before long I'm running around laughing
as I bite at the snow
my black hair now white
I breathe out
it becomes ice.
I'm moving faster
Toshie joins in barking
together we make a joyous pair.
The buildings change
as they're covered in snow
snow blankets
uniformity ensues.

Time seems stilled.

Hello Sunshine

Hello sunshine
you came and beguiled the rain
met Joe Starling and Bo Rook
but don't crow about it.
Dip below
be lost from view
but warm the blood of gators and toads
refresh vintage fruits as we gather their yield
drink in your rays, becoming robust.

Yellow Bird

Yellow bird soaring skywards
spun a loop hurled down divine
intoxicated she sang gladly
her ribs reverberated in time
she felt euphoric.
Sublime.

The Gilt Mirror

The gilt mirror reflected it hadn't been true
Dave was not fat
as she had shown
but hey, mirrors have troubles too.

Like relationship woes
so she distorted the truth
because she could.
So take heed my people
gilt-edged mirrors are so just the limit
self-centred, looking in on themselves with self-love
so be afraid
very afraid.

Am I a Fish?

Cool water holding me
trusting, I relax
drop down
a shimmering light beckons
stealthily I swim closer
stillness covers me like a fog
as questions arise.
Have I become one with the sea?
Have I evolved becoming fish?
As I flip freely, wriggling down deep
tranquillity encircles me
my feet flap, wishing they had wings
my senses are awash
I spurt forth
bliss descends
calm.

In the Face of Madness (Age Five)

In the face of madness
I ate courage
it tasted
sweet
soured the insanity of
the Holy ones.

contradicted their rage.
Courage covered me like a blanket
warming my mind, keeping their
icy words at bay
words that attacked my soul.

Courage felled the nuns
struck back at their brutal kicks
heavy blows.
So I tightened its blanket
around my tiny frame.

I cried tears that exhausted me
which no one saw or heard.
But I ate courage till I was
full and freed in time
in the face of madness, I ate
courage
it tasted sweet.

Guardian Moon

The Moon sailed across the attic
lighting up shadows, muttering quietly
afraid to wake you as its beam
played around your pillow
resting on your face.
She whispered love poems while stroking your hair
you stirred
she retreats
knowing you're safe.

A Moon Morning

Today the sun melled
with the moon
presented itself in a
circle of iridescent light
hummed nonchalantly in its
splendid veil.

A moon morning
with crisp edges of night
an owl hooted as the cock crowed
slumber turned
around.

Babies stirred
sensing it was
time
to suck breast
on this moon morn.

Ti Amo Rain

Rain, Oh bella bella rain
raining down
falling sideways
aided by the wind
tree branches bow
sister trees bow back.
But still you pour
nourishing the soil
for seeds to flourish.

Oh wonderful rain
decanting down
delightfully
to benefit us all
rain.
Oh ti amo rain.

Fly or Die

Trapped on a ledge
fingers scraping
the wall
no sounds escape from
jaws clamped tight
tension grips
like an overstrung
cello about to snap.

His back buckles
he is losing control
his feet slide
over he goes
piercing screams
render the air.
I wonder if he died
or flew?

Happy

Happy to be
no worries
no frowns.
Happy to be
smiling inside.
Happy to be
alive.

Happily Drowning
(in Crete)

Happily drowning
I sink slowly
sounds disappear
I'm falling further
dress billows out
I care less.

I'm happily drowning
slipping into this
azul world
where translucent fish
flash by.
Earth forgotten
hazy memories leak out
and swim away.

I don't stop them
I'm content, trusting
weightless
a serene figure
rolling over and
over.

With the rippling waves
lingering on the crest
my hair like fronds
streams out
I drift away emitting hums
happily drowning.

Dangling Legs
(in Stromness)

I observe dangling legs
swirling against the dock
as the murky waters
sweep past.

A young girl
sits hunched over
despair permeates the air
a thirteenth birthday card lies
shredded.

I approach stealthily
gagging from the
stench of her unwashed clothes
while listening to her deep sobs.

I reach her
crouch down low
whispering
'Can I help?'

Cherubs' Needs

The reluctant cherubs
waited and waited
impatience stencilled
around their mouths
they were butt-naked
innocence
chins resting on
folded arms
disquiet danced
around their eyes
yet sweetly they rest
fingers in mouths
eyes raised
pleading to be released.

Wings twitching
telling tales
of torment and exasperation
please, please let us go!
Oh no! Wet legs!

Rainbow Hands
(in Princes Street)

There's a rainbow on this brown hand
the clarity is sharp
rich and supreme.

It filtered through the window
a present from the rain
when it was done
it slipped away.

But wait –
my rainbow's back
more vivid like
juicy limes, watermelons
red.

The rainbow gave itself to me.
I rejoice that it chose
these brown hands
writing poems
in its honour.

Trust

A goddess stood on my
window ledge
waiting, watching,
I stared back.

She looked splendid
in a shimmering
haze of colours
eyes piercing, radiating
love and compassion.

Asking, not demanding,
she waited, I stuttered
I'm scared – have doubts.

'I know, my precious one.
If I hold out my hand
can you bear to touch
the tip of my finger?
Trust me, take a small step.'

I hesitated, shook,
tears rained down,
trembling, my left leg

dropped to the floor.
I took a step,
my body
followed.

Tentatively I stretched out my arm,
my fingertips searching
for her hand
our fingers met.

Intense heat seared
through my body,
I collapsed, falling
forwards.

She caught me gently in her
arms,
soothing my aching limbs,
wiping away my tears.

She loved me unconditionally.
I knew
I believed
I was
at peace.

Morning Delight

She woke up delighted
sun shining brightly
she pirouetted around the
floor.
Laughing and singing
she skipped along the road
carefree content
ignoring the stares
keeping away from the
lions and snares
chortling loudly
she flung her arms
in the air
backflipped over and over
for as long as she dared.

Which was forever
because she didn't
really give a hoot.

He Threw the Dice

He threw the
dice to start his life
today he threw a six
six attempts to get it
right
six things to do or not
write six poems
or six songs
he pondered for
six seconds –
who cared?
he could always
throw the dice again
and again
and again.

Today is not a good day (definitely not)

In a café sat a woman
she sneezed
her tooth flew out
caught on reflex
hidden in her purse
lips clenched to hide the
gap.

No smiling today
because today is not a
good day
(definitely not!).
A stranger smiled over
she turned her head to the
wall.

A man asked to join her
she gave him the evil eye
then curled herself
around her cup
giving off bad vibes
knowing
today is not a good day
(definitely not!).

She muttered to herself
 'I loathe everything,'
a waiter enquired,
'is Madam well?'
She threw him a caustic glance
and the milk turned sour
she was exceedingly pleased
because
today was not a good day
(definitely not!).

Wet Socks in Leith

A cloudburst soaks
the dim-lit streets
as shadows flash by
keeping their owners
a secret in the rain.
Rain creating pools
for feet to flounder
in or avoid
while a girl in
a billowing cape
heads into an unseen pool
drowning her socks.

Demented Ironing Board

The chair slid across
the deck
like a demented ironing board
on hash
the non-sailors scuttled
like bankers to
the other side.

Shooting out liquid
reminiscent of a
fountain
containing bits.

Sulphur-scented Haggis

Sulphur-scented haggis
sizzling on the grill
the bouquet shoots
through my aorta
like rapids on heat
I choke spluttering
liquid
like a fire hydrant
gone green.

What on Earth Happened?
(in Mallaig)

Sun hat drooped
obscures your eyes
you shuffle along
body morphing into
a swaying blot.
I ponder, exclaiming silently
what on earth happened?

Did someone steal your soul?
Your carefree ways?
When did you lose
your laughing child?
Teenage swag?
Where is the young woman
full of plans?
I wish I could
return your soul
wrapped in gold.

But hey!
Pull off your hat
shake that hair
loose

start to sway
shimmy and dance
then it will come back tenfold!

Screaming in Ecstasy

Rich earth enfold me
cover my body
beneath your soil
let me taste your sweetness
let me drink in your
smoked scent which
wafts around my senses.
I dream you in
while compost trickles
down my spine
leaving leaf imprints.
My mind unfurls.

Dropping used notes
as a melody of
thoughts drift in.
Birthing fresh songs
sucked from your centre
my body writhes
shifting worms
and scurrying things
beetles are sheltering
up my nose.
Mirth reaches my lips

every orifice is full
full of movement
I twist and turn as soil
falls into my eyes
I cry out – I am all yours
good earth!

We are no longer separate –
we've become one!
Flinching, I start
to spin furiously
screaming in ecstasy
whirling like a vortex
I erupt!
Shoot out of the ground
uprooting trees
overturning stones
till I land naked
rebirthed
shiny anew.

Warm and Toasty
(in Princes Street)

Seated in a warm café
retreating from the rain
sipping chai
froth so nice
in my mouth.
I take a sip
and savour the flavour
as it glides
down my throat.
I gloat
warming my hands
on the mug
I stare through
the window
spy a castle
getting soaked.
While me, toasty
snug within
this noisy hub
drooling over cakes
but don't partake.
How good is that?
Now I'm dozing, bum unfrozen
curled up and homey in my easy chair.

Tiny Blue Flower

Summer's closed its door
autumn's sweeping past
wintery sun gone down
yet a tiny blue flower
remains in bloom
I ask it 'why?'
She replies

'I ride on alternate seasons
I live a new note
which saves me from
the harsh winds,
the sleet and snow.
Join me if you're bold.'

Ghost Trees

The forest has sumptuous
textures
rough as dogs' teeth
while fungi grow
soft as down
where leaves tumble
crisp in death

a once vibrant forest
becomes bare stark
like a thousand
ghost trees
luminous in the
moonlight.

No End Road

I placed one foot down
then another
no looking back
staying on track
while the wind howled
I screened my eyes
from its dust
down came the rain
swept me back
I straggled on
dripping rivers
a crevice opened up
I stumbled in
clutching at rocks
shoes slid off
I lunged at the sides
pulling up hard
strode on shoeless
staying on track
no looking back.

Then popped into Greggs for a snack.

The Moon in Brazil

Moonlight on a Brazil shore
me dipping in toes
perched on a log
as the waves lap songs
I feel caught inside
their sounds
sounds that unscramble
my worries, my brain.

I'm lulled into an
internal silence
as coconuts bob over
the horizon, floating
to the shore
giving away nothing
how they got to this
paradise island.

A breeze stirs – palm
trees click their leaves
still the water comes
curling under my feet,
seeping between my toes.

I stir little, caught in reflection
of the moon in Brazil.

Wise Woman

Ancient woman in the
chic laundrette
shuffling forward
sorting, folding
piles of clothes
is it you?
Are you the ubiquitous elder
who transforms through
the ages
to become.
Is it you?

Is it you?
I may have glimpsed
before
in London, Paris
Delhi –
is it you?
Everywhere doing onerous
tasks
that others won't do
ancient woman in the
chic laundrette.
Is this your ultimate path?

We thank you!

The VIP Letter

Dropped my schoolbag
on the floor
threw myself onto
the bed
pulled my pillow tightly
over my head
just to think
to erase the school day
and everyone over twelve
I want to learn
something that really matters
not geog or trig
I care about justice
I want to strike out
write a letter
to those in charge
I don't care if they can't
don't read my letter
as long as I wrote it
I know I cared.

The Fringe Festival

You came excited, expecting
drawn away from your lives.
You come to experience the dream
a fantasy of performances
laughter and queues
two hours of illusion
emptying your mind
of bills and Pete
the litter tray
the quarrels
you're thrilled
people yakking
atmosphere buzzing.

The makeup covers your
black eye
smile, it's fun, two hours
away from the dog crap
the cold 'cause your power
card's run out.
Music blares, jokes come
fast

but you forget behind
the painted masks
lie lives full of shit,
bills to pay, Jane to avoid.

Two sets of people, playing a game of illusions.

Creatures

Something stirred in the gloom
he stood statuesque,
bones frozen like ice.
His throat drowned
in its own saliva
the creature scuttled
from side to side
edging ever closer
its red eyes glowed.

Suddenly it launched
itself
sticking its claws deep into
his skin
the pain woke him from his stupor
he pushed and shoved
eventually punching it
between the eyes
then running for dear life
not stopping till he was
many miles away.

Today

Today I sat quiet as a rose
before sleep
its soft petals stroking
my skin like a mink brush
in the stillness I heard a faint
tinkle.
God was whispering her
love
and I bowed in thanks.

Today I woke up

Today I woke up and the sun shone
over me
I blinked awake
arose from my tender repose
then started to sway
dance
threw my hands high,
swirled around
listening to the divine
beating within my heart
we were as one –
in love.

Suck Out the Juice

The pyramid of oranges
appealed to my gut
I wanted to savour
then devour
suck out the juices
extract the life
from these tangy spheres
let the nectar
dribble from my mouth
stain my robes
let the juice roam free
drop into infinity with
panache
and a soundless splash
cool satisfaction.

Ice Tea

Ice tea
slipping down my gullet
like a moving glacier
rushing through
the cavern of my
inners
keeping them coolly
hydrated.

Visions of Scotland

Free Scotland
fresh ideas
free parking
nae sanctions
on yer cash
affordable housing
austerity ending
quality of life extending
refugees welcome
economy rising
greed dying
green energy blooming
fish exports flying
prosperity high
is a republic nigh?
Freed Scotland.

Winking Fairy

The tree undressed
baubles and tinsel
shimmied to the floor
beaded garlands
tiny bells snaked between branches
sounding a musical
clink
lights untwisting
determined to cling on
in knots.

The star, the penultimate one
to go
shone large in its
decadent descent
leaving the fairy atop
raucously laughing
dancing her way
down the tree
glitter cascading from her
crumpled dress
she lands with a crash
a cheeky wink
sipping a thimble of drink.

Night Market in Lagos

We Nigerians have sharp elbows
useful for pushing onto buses
or gaining access to the night market
lit by candles sat in tins
throwing out warm shadows
while wooden corrals hold
in the heaving mass.

Tables laden with meat carcasses
that lie tightly bound
prodded by the crowd as
they sidle past
weaving the bright radiant
fabrics between sweaty palms
as they peruse a myriad of colourful
bargains heaped high.

Greens, fruit lie strewn over stalls
ideal to grasp
succulent papaya
draws in the people
as grain pours over
the table's edge
like rain.
A tiny boy screams

he's scooped up
it's no place to be trodden
underfoot
unseen, this seething
throng move as one
the quiet ship sails on
undisturbed by teeth whistles
the scent of catfish stew

their minds focused
only on what they need
or as far as a Naira
will stretch
a river of murmurs flow
among the cast
as they trail as one
to the exit and leave
elbows sharpened, ready
to propel-ram ourselves onto the buses
and win those coveted seats.

Girl Power

When I was a girl
I learned to be quiet,
smile and please,
wash the dishes
while my brothers played.
Today as a woman
I've learned to use my
voice to be loud,
leave the dishes,
play and please myself.

What is a Logophile?

I'm a logophile
I love words'
capacity to be sumptuous
and scalding
I'm enchanted by their
ability to express
both tender and devilish
prose
writing is adventurous but
laden with fears
taking you to
dangerous and exhilarating
heights
where you can be swallowed up
or rewarded with shiny praise
take a risk
write now
live life to the max
be a nerd, the world loves nerds.

Nazareth House
(Prison Aged Six)

She lies rigid, afraid to breathe
in case it starts
so thin her ribs stick out
large wounds ooze yellow pus
from crusted sores which
she nibbles on
feet bleed, staining the coarse sheets
while her hair moves en masse
the lice feeding on the dirt
she whimpers quietly
afraid of what may happen next.

Soundless, the nuns creep in
drag her from her bed and hack off her
hair in an upstairs room
returning, the small girls weeps
feeling crushed
hoping to die before morning
before the nuns start the beatings
again.

Obama Inauguration

Obama you did it
did it for me
for the world.

Dear Barack,
I am so proud of you
the world has changed
forever
today, tomorrow
nothing can be the same
we, your black and white voters,
can now love ourselves
even in Britain we feel the acceptance
the coming down of the curtain of racism
the blanket of deceit has been removed
white and black can see each other
more clearly
that we are all human with the same
pains, dreams, hopes and aspirations
Obama, I don't know if you realise
the enormity of what's happened
today.

It symbolises for me that anybody
irrespective of their colour can achieve
and will achieve
as you have reached the highest
office in your land
that may now transfer
to other nations.
I today cannot express
the depth of my feelings
you have freed me from
the prison of oppression
I can breathe more easily
the burden has been lessened
in my lifetime
I have now experienced hope as a black
citizen of the world
I may now be a part of it
my children are free.
Free to be.

You, Barack, are the mirror
we all cried for but did not realise for what
but today we know
all black and white people
know of hope
new possibilities, change

nothing can stop this momentum
the door can no longer be kept closed
it has been blown open.

President Obama,
your success has allowed us black citizens to be counted in with the human race
and for that I am truly humbled.

Bring Back Our Girls

bring back our girls
three hundred held
all clothed in grey
mouths sealed
but open
hearts quake with thoughts
too dark
wishing they were home
with family
playing with friends,
at school safe

bring back our girls
three hundred held
but the media departs
fresh headlines a new day
our girls forgotten

bring back our girls
three hundred held
some impregnated
bring back our girls
help now

The Glassy Loch

The glassy loch reflects a double sky
casting mirrored images
upon the sky
I gasp
at this ethereal sight
harbouring snow-capped
mountains within its grasp
breathless, I sink down
trying to digest
this optical feast
my eyes become a spring
and I cry.

Shy Love's Blush

When you say I love you
I blush knowing it might be true
yet so afraid it's another
who looks just like me!

Hurrah I'm in the club

Hurrah I'm in the club –
it's only taken thirty years to a lifetime.
Hurrah I'm in the club, fully paid up membership
our mixed race shared heritage as a plus!
Valued, vindicated by who? You, them
the UN, a special year
so we can be seen, heard, taken on board
what took so long?
We've known for years we're fabulous, fantastic
gloriously awesome, leading in the world
...

We rock, we roll as ambassadors of nations
respected, listened to, sought after, read.
We teach, educate, are storytellers, poets –
Like role models we shine in the gloom of this depression.
No need for a special date but we'll take it and run with it
celebrating peoples of African descent.
Gie us the funds, we have the ideas.
The flair, to set up schools, debates, write plays
develop art
our energy knows no bounds; we are on fire!
Our intellect burns bright
we're not afraid to take the first leap in the dark.

So we will take this year and celebrate in style.
We have been on the frontline in past times
women like Harriet Tubman who spoke our truths
we are sisters of sojourner truth.
We have hundreds of sheroes and heroes,
chiefs and wise ones to learn from.
None shied away when things got tough,
by threats of enslavement and being shot.

We marched forward as today
our leading lights, Kelly Holmes, Zadie Smith and others
across the world you'll find us riding high, enjoying great success before this allotted year
but don't worry, we'll take it and run
setting the world ablaze
even though we've faced discrimination
been attacked and killed.

We still hold our heads high with dignity and self-respect
we celebrate every year and every day we're alive!
So thanks UN for giving us this year
us people of African descent
so let's party on down and cheer and cheer and cheer
big it up for us people of African descent.

Dreamscape Melts

Dreamscape as succulent as cherries
that blossom in my honeyed slumber
inspiring waves of music
tinkling within a temple
with me swathed in royal silks
in deep sea blues
melting.

Some other books published by **Luath Press**

Bad Ass Raindrop
Kokumo Rocks
ISBN 1 84282 018 4 PBK £6.99

What would happen if a raindrop took acid? Does your bum shake and does your belly wobble? And have you noticed that there are no black babies on 'New Baby' cards?

Fadeke Kokumo Rocks' poetry is alive with love, passion, humour and brutal honesty. It is sharply observed, potent and insightful, capturing beautifully the sixth dimension of the creative eye. It has a rich diversity of time and content which embraces the globe and its conflicts, domestic and urban.

You can hear the monsoon rains of Africa, taste the mangoes of India, touch the compassion and spirit of the child and sense the pain of burning flesh as race riots rage. Full of Kokumo's distinctive humour, *Bad Ass Raindrop* challenges the questions we answer unquestioning.

Stolen from Africa
Kokumo Rocks
ISBN 978 190630 719 6 PBK £7.99

Kokumo's second collection of poetry explores love, race, nature, freedom and imprisonment, with fun and humour.

Alternating between the luscious natural world and feelings of war and anger, Kokumo's poetry takes the reader from resolution to conflict, then back again. Taught in schools across Scotland, her work helps children attain an appreciation for poetry and Black History.

The Tiger Woods of performance poetry. ANGUS CALDER

Details of these and other books published by Luath Press can be found at:
www.luath.co.uk

Luath Press Limited

committed to publishing well written books worth reading

LUATH PRESS takes its name from Robert Burns, whose little collie Luath (*Gael.*, swift or nimble) tripped up Jean Armour at a wedding and gave him the chance to speak to the woman who was to be his wife and the abiding love of his life. Burns called one of the 'Twa Dogs' Luath after Cuchullin's hunting dog in Ossian's *Fingal*. Luath Press was established in 1981 in the heart of Burns country, and is now based a few steps up the road from Burns' first lodgings on Edinburgh's Royal Mile. Luath offers you distinctive writing with a hint of unexpected pleasures.

Most bookshops in the UK, the US, Canada, Australia, New Zealand and parts of Europe, either carry our books in stock or can order them for you. To order direct from us, please send a £sterling cheque, postal order, international money order or your credit card details (number, address of cardholder and expiry date) to us at the address below. Please add post and packing as follows: UK – £1.00 per delivery address; overseas surface mail – £2.50 per delivery address; overseas airmail – £3.50 for the first book to each delivery address, plus £1.00 for each additional book by airmail to the same address. If your order is a gift, we will happily enclose your card or message at no extra charge.

Luath Press Limited
543/2 Castlehill
The Royal Mile
Edinburgh EH1 2ND
Scotland
Telephone: +44 (0)131 225 4326 (24 hours)
Email: sales@luath. co.uk
Website: www. luath.co.uk